PATH OF WONDER

ALSO BY ELLEN GRACE O'BRIAN

the Jewel of Abundance:
Finding Prosperity through the Ancient Wisdom of Yoga

Living the Eternal Way:
Spiritual Meaning and Practice for Daily Life

A Single Blade of Grass:
Finding the Sacred in Everyday Life

Living for the Sake of the Soul

The Moon Reminded Me

One Heart Opening

The Sanctuary of Belonging

Once Before Time

A Day of Silence

PATH OF WONDER

A MEDITATOR'S GUIDE TO ADVENT

ELLEN GRACE O'BRIAN

CSE Press
San Jose, California

Cover and Interior Design: Irma Lovic
Cover Photography: Unsplash

CSE Press
1146 University Avenue
San Jose, California, 95126
+1 408 283 0221
csepress@csecenter.org
www.CSEcenter.org

For all those
who yearn for the awakened life
and will not settle for less.

Contents

Introduction

The divine manifestation is ubiquitous; only our eyes are not open to it.
The symbol opens our eyes.
— Joseph Campbell

To traverse a path in the dark night, we walk carefully, carry a lamp, or orient our way by the moon or starlight. When there is no such light to guide us, we grow quiet and profoundly aware. We listen deeply and find our way with the inner light of mindful awareness, deeply attuned to the now moment. One step at a time, the way forward is revealed.

Spiritual practices imbued with symbols from the Christian tradition of Advent can be luminous tools to guide us through the dark days and nights of Winter. Through contemplation and meditation, we prepare our hearts and minds to reach what yogis call *Kutastha Chaitanya*—realization of the universal Christ or Krishna Consciousness—the unchanging, eternal, divine Self of all. During the Christmas season, many homes have evergreen trees laden with lights and gifts, and doors or tables display wreaths and candles, often without connection to the ancient power such symbols carry. When that occurs, what could facilitate transformation in a dark season and bring us to the heart of spiritual realization serves only to decorate our home. While these customs often provide a context for valuable family traditions and social connections, they could offer so much more.

When I first read Paramahansa Yogananda's seminal book, *Autobiography of a Yogi*, I was captivated by the wealth of references to scriptures connecting East and West in the deep stream of mysticism. The ancient cry of the Rig Veda, "Truth is one; sages refer to it variously," resonated with my intuitive sense that one Absolute Reality expresses in the world's religions and spiritual traditions. Just as millions of people worldwide, regardless of religious belief, benefit from yoga's philosophy and practices, so can we benefit from learning about, exploring, and experiencing various traditions of the world's religions. In today's religiously pluralistic world, such encounters are becoming commonplace. How we approach those encounters makes all the difference to our spiritual development.

Exploring and experiencing the practices of a religion or spiritual tradition different from one's own requires both respect and humility. As strangers to a tradition (or, in some cases, exiles from it), we must approach that mysterious doorway with respect for it as an opening to a divine encounter, along with the awareness that our understanding is limited. A willing heart and an open mind are significant support to seekers of spiritual truth.

Paramahansa Yogananda wrote: *It is of utmost importance to all people, whatever their religion, that they experience within themselves the "birth" of the Universal Christ.* How are we to encourage that birth? In simple terms, we make ourselves ready for it. We decide we will enter the season as a spiritual pilgrim. We prepare for the journey by study, contemplation, prayer, meditation, and opening to the story's symbols and the season's transformative potential.

This daily contemplative guide supports the spiritual journey of Advent for pilgrims from all traditions. The meaning of Advent is "coming or arrival." It signifies the period of faithful waiting for the birth of the Universal Christ—realization of the essential divine Self. What could such spiritual awakening make possible in our lives and our world?

May this season welcome the light that dispels the darkness of ignorance, the light that brings peace to all the world.

How to Use This Daily Guide for Advent

Only wonder comprehends. —Gregory of Nyssa

Many blessings to you as you begin this contemplative pilgrimage during the Advent season! May the radiance of your essence of being light your path through the darkness of unknowing, and may wonder bloom in the depths of your heart as you encounter the great mystery of the divine Self.

This daily guide for contemplation will support mindful awareness each day. The inspirational readings, scriptures, practices, and questions for reflection serve as an asana—a steady seat for that day, and that day only. Just as the most useful meditation asana is firm and intentional and relaxed and open, so is the best approach to daily devotion during Advent. We cultivate faithful waiting. We refrain from the temptation to read ahead and try to accomplish the mission. The mission is to wait, to wonder, and stay open to the inner light of inspiration and guidance.

Meditate every day. Keep an Advent journal. Write your response to the daily questions and note what you are feeling, questioning, struggling with, or celebrating.

Perhaps not all the practices will appeal to you. Feel free to skip them but write about that. Note why you were not inclined or decided not to engage. After each of the four weeks of Advent, read through your journal entries. Indicate the themes you see and any insight that dawns during your review.

Advent always begins on the fourth Sunday before Christmas. Due to the changing position of December 25th with the previous Sunday, the number of days marked during the Advent season will vary. Some Advent guides conclude with Christmas Eve, and others with Christmas Day. The changing dates of each calendar year also affect the specific day of the week that precedes Christmas. You can read the entry for that weekday first, and then add the entry for Christmas Eve and Christmas Day as is appropriate.

Each Sunday in the season marks a new beginning or deepening of the contemplative journey. If you use an Advent wreath, you will light a candle each Sunday, signifying that juncture.

Supports for Your Journey

An Advent Journal

Use a physical or digital journal dedicated to this contemplative four-week pilgrimage.

An Advent Wreath

You can make a simple Advent wreath with five candles and candleholders (or a plate if you use votives). Instead of hanging on a mantle or door, the Advent wreath sits on a table, altar, or another flat surface. One candle occupies the center of the circle; this represents Christ Consciousness. Four additional candles form a circle around it. In the Christian tradition, depending on the particular denomination, the four candles are specific colors—often three purple and one pink signifying qualities of the journey. The central candle is usually white. Feel free to choose the colors and qualities that will mark your pilgrimage, such as blue for willingness, purple for devotion, yellow for surrender, and so forth. Pray about it. Write about it. Decide what the four markers of your journey will be. If you are a Kriya yogi, you can draw from the *yamas* and *niyamas*—nonviolence or compassion, truth, purity, contentment, surrender, or any that are right for you at this time.

Traditionally, one lights the Christ candle at the conclusion of the journey—on Christmas Eve or Christmas Day. However, I have found it useful to kindle it first, each time a new week begins, as a reminder to me of the omnipresent Spirit ever guiding my journey. Light the candle from the previous week or weeks before illuminating the one for the new week. All the lights will burn bright at the conclusion of your journey.

Nativity Images

If you have a nativity set, this is the time to get it out and set it up where you can see it. If it is not something you have, you don't need to purchase one. There are many images of the nativity in artwork that you can access on the web. Search and see what captures your attention. It would be useful to print one out and place it in your journal to look at with each day's contemplation.

THE COSMIC CHRIST

WEEK ONE

Awakening to Christ Consciousness is beholding the One in all. Compassion is its natural expression.

First Sunday: The Art of Waiting

Today begins the intentional discipline of faithful waiting—cultivating a positive expectancy that heightens our sensitivity to life. Working with the symbols of Advent is a useful way to experience greater spiritual depth in the days before us. The Christmas story is replete with themes of watching and waiting. Mary is expecting. Joseph waits for inner guidance. The shepherds watch their flocks at night. The wise men search the stars for direction. Through watching and waiting, the miraculous journey unfolds.

So much in Western culture encourages more activity, not less, during the days leading up to Christmas. In the US, this particular time is heralded as the most important shopping occasion of the year. What a stark contrast to the inner call to contemplation. In the past, people camped out in front of shops to be the first in line when the store opens at midnight. That was superseded by Black Friday online specials to kickstart the season. Shop, correspond with family and friends, finish year-end work projects, plan special meals and online parties, decorate your home, and on it goes. It is no wonder that so many arrive at Christmas weary of all of the activity, hype, and lack of substance that truly inspires. Yet, when approached with spiritual discipline, these days hold great promise that can enrich not only our inner life but our time of festivity with family and friends as well. The rise of a global pandemic had us all examine how to reinvent our holiday celebrations. We don't have to choose either contemplation or activity. A spiritual focus can help us set the right priorities.

Let's begin with the commitment to engage in contemplation during this time, deepen our meditation practice, and reflect on the universal spiritual themes that this season of divine revelation can offer. Along with your regular prayer and meditation time, use these daily guides to explore the spiritual meaning of this season. Approach it with anticipation of divine grace unfolding.

Practice:

Many of us these days are not so skilled at waiting. We are used to speed and become impatient with slow computers or long lines. We want what we want now because our minds are already onto the next thing. Add to that the presence of ongoing, pervasive stress in life. Our tempers may be short and attention distracted. The art of waiting is the skill of remaining in the moment, right where we are, and considering that moment precious. How do we do that? We do it by watching and witnessing when our attention wanders off into the past or into some imagined future.

When our thoughts veer into the future, we miss the present moment. Now becomes nothing more than a link between where we are and where we want to be. But now is where *life* is. The present moment is where we find God; it is the only time we can truly connect with ourselves and one another. The good news is that when we notice our attention running from the now, we are already stepping back into being present. Just notice that. Then be aware of your breath. Imagine that whatever the moment is, that moment is alive with God. This return to being present now comprises the art of waiting.

Contemplate:

Waiting patiently in expectation is the foundation of the spiritual life.
—Simone Weil

Now yoga (conscious oneness) is explained. Yoga is experienced when thought activity is restrained. The seer then abides in its own (divine) nature. —Patanjali's Yoga Sutra 1.1-3

Keep awake, therefore, for you do not know on what day your Lord is coming. —Matthew 24:42

Reflect:

How willing am I to remain in the moment? What must I let go of to be fully here? What happens when I turn my attention to the breath?

Monday: Possibility

It's been a while since I set up a nativity scene in our home during Advent. Over the decades, a few nativity sets have come and gone—lost in moves or passed on to others. This year I decided to purchase a new one online. I selected one that includes the animals mentioned in scripture and the central figures of Mary, Joseph, the infant Jesus, angels, shepherds, and wise men.

The qualities that each figure in the nativity can represent, including all the animals, captivates my attention. What does each one bring to mind? What feeling does it elicit? To consider the nativity scene as symbolic of our inner qualities can be inspiring and yield surprising insights.

When the new nativity set arrived, and I unpacked it piece by piece, I was delighted with the figures' artistry. When I got to the last compartment and removed a little standing lamb, I noticed its back leg was broken. I could have sent it back. But as I held the tiny figure, I was aware that I did not want to return it. I wanted to repair it. With a little carpenter's glue, some careful alignment and pressure, the lamb was once again able to stand.

I am not sure why the lamb with the broken leg appealed to me. Yet, I know that it can be useful to follow the heart and attend to what it reveals. Repairing the lamb's leg, I remembered a story of Ramakrishna, who served as temple priest at Dakshineswar. When another priest moved Krishna's image, he accidentally dropped it and broke one of the legs. It is considered inappropriate to worship a damaged image. The local Pandits recommended discarding the broken icon in the Ganges and creating a new one for the temple. When they consulted Ramakrishna, he said if one's child had a broken leg, it would be natural to seek healing, not look for another child. He advised approaching this situation in the same way. Ramakrishna himself repaired the statue so skillfully that the break was not apparent, and the statue was restored to its former function.

One of the great promises of the Advent of Christ Consciousness is healing. The ego limits, divides, and turns away from imperfection, but Christ Consciousness reveals wholeness and brings healing amid brokenness. What was once considered impossible becomes possible with God. During the days of Advent, cultivate a greater receptivity to healing.

Practice:

Set aside some contemplative time to view a representation of the nativity. Instead of seeing the scene as depicting something historical or even mythological, explore it as symbolic of your innate wholeness, containing the myriad qualities that exist within us all. Perhaps you see the strength (or stubbornness) of the ox, docility of the sheep, the devotion of the shepherd, or receptivity of the manger. Include everything you see and note what it stirs in your heart and mind. This contemplation of nativity scenes can be done with three-dimensional sets, with art images in books or online, or through our imagination as we read scriptural accounts of the Christmas story.

As you contemplate the nativity scene, look at each part individually. What do you notice? Notice what comes to mind. What feelings are present? See if there is any part of the scene that captures your attention. Be curious about it. Write about it.

Contemplate:

Christ has ever abided in me. He has preached through my consciousness to all my rowdy and hypocritical thoughts...I was mentally blind, my will was lame; but I was healed by the awakened Christ in me.
—Paramahansa Yogananda

The wolf also shall dwell with the lamb, and the leopard shall lie down with the kid; and the calf and the young lion and the fatling together; and a little child shall lead them. —Isaiah 11.5-6

Reflect:

Am I open to healing? Are there situations, relationships, or conditions in my life ready to be healed or transformed? Is there one step toward healing I can take today?

Tuesday: The Cosmic Christ

The spiritual message of Christmas is the call for everyone to awaken to their divine identity. A child is born! New life is given as we are born in the realization of truth, love, and freedom—*as we awaken to our true nature.*

This new life has requirements and makes demands upon us. We must be willing to grow, open our hearts and minds, and release old ideas not consistent with truth. Paramahansa Yogananda said, "To bring divine awareness into our human consciousness, we must outgrow the limited conventional concept of Christ." The limited concept of Christ would have us believe only Jesus represents the Christ of God. Some even imagine that Christ is Jesus' last name. The limited view suggests that the coming of Christ is purely a historic event that we celebrate at Christmas, December 25th, a day designated as Jesus' birthday.

For many Christians, the word Christ is synonymous with Jesus and refers to the Messiah prophesied in the Hebrew Scriptures. The word Christ means the Anointed one—sanctified through the anointing of oil. The mystical meaning of anointing is the revelation of divine truth, which brings the liberation of consciousness from all limiting belief systems. The revelation of spiritual truth is often accompanied by an energetic opening of the crown chakra—thus, a mystical "anointing" coincides with awakening to the inner Christ. The omnipresent Christ is the life of God within us. That life is eternal.

The Christ Spirit was fully realized and manifested in Jesus. His life and teachings demonstrate the light of Christ Consciousness, God's anointed one, the Self- and God-realized man. What can we see when we read the scriptural accounts and contemplate his awakened consciousness and teachings? When we really look, we can see evidence of unconditional love and unadulterated and uncompromising truth.

When we are of the Christ mind, we realize our divine origin, birth, and nature. We recognize it in everyone. Awakening to Christ Consciousness is beholding the One in all. Compassion is its natural expression.

Practice:

Enter into meditation by turning your attention within and acknowledging God's omnipresence. Inwardly affirm that you are meditating in God, know that the life of God is expressing as you.

Once your attention has become interiorized, direct it to the root chakra at the base of your spine. Progressively move your attention and awareness through each of the seven major chakras or energy centers. From the root chakra, move awareness to the second center below the navel, then to the third below the diaphragm, followed by the fourth opposite the heart, the fifth at the throat, the sixth at the spiritual eye (between and above the eyebrows) and then let your awareness rest at the crown chakra, just beyond the top of the head.

As you conclude your meditation, imagine light or energy emanating from your crown chakra. Imagine, feel, and affirm that the inner light of Christ Consciousness is permeating your mind and body. Then bring your attention back to your environment and affirm that you are spiritually awake and established in truth. Before you end your session, share your experience of peace and well-being with others. Intentionally offer loving-kindness to people everywhere. Inwardly agree to behold the One in all.

Contemplate:

It is of utmost importance to all people, whatever their religion, that they experience within themselves this "birth" of the Universal Christ.
—Paramahansa Yogananda

The historical Jesus was one man, and Christ is not his last name. The Christ includes the whole sweep of creation and history joined with him —and you too. We call this the Cosmic Christ. —Fr. Richard Rohr

Reflect:

Are there ideas that I hold about the Christ that I must outgrow? What are those ideas based on? Am I open to new insight? What does a new understanding require of me?

Wednesday: To Hope Once More

December stillness
prayers reach down
into darkness
like winter roots.
Underground
they grow branches
weave shadow nests
for the winged life
of our dreams.
—Ellen Grace O'Brian

Our ability to be open and hopeful is directly related to our willingness to trust God, to trust that our Higher Power is, indeed, abundantly good. Perhaps we have trained ourselves not to hope or expect too much in order to avoid potential disappointment. To protect ourselves from the suffering of disappointment, it may seem safer not to risk hoping. Yet we pay for that kind of safety with our joy and our enthusiasm for life. It takes tremendous effort to dampen down the Spirit within which hope continually rises.

Hope is essential to our spiritual journey. It is the expression of our innate yearning to realize God. Within everyone is the deepest hope to know eternal life, experience unconditional joy, and be completely aware. To hope to experience life, bliss, and awareness without limits is to yearn to realize our essential unbounded Self. The soul naturally yearns to know God. Paramahansa Yogananda explained that we must want God with such intensity that we feel we cannot wait another day. Yet, if the realization does not come, we must be willing to wait with fervent hope.

Advent invites us to consider opening ourselves to hope once again, dream dreams in the darkness to be celebrated in the light, be ready to enter the mystery surrounding us, lose the false self, and find our essential Self anew.

Practice:

To hope is to expect, to anticipate, or look forward to. Cultivate a hopeful attitude by assuming there is a Power for good in this universe, and you are choosing to cooperate with It.

Feel or imagine that life supports you. Expect that divine grace, God's freely given support, is at work in your life in seen and unseen ways. Notice what it is like to consciously choose to be hopeful.

Contemplate:

To hope means to be ready
At every moment
For that which is not yet born,
And yet not become desperate
If there is no birth in our lifetime.
There is no sense in hoping
For that which already exists
Or for that which cannot be.
Those whose hope is weak
Settle down for comfort or for violence;
Those whose hope is strong
See and cherish all signs of new life
And are ready every moment
To help the birth
Of that which is ready to be born.
—Erich Fromm from *The Revolution of Hope*

Reflect:

What does hope mean to you? Is it a part of your life today?

Ask yourself: Can I allow myself to be genuinely hopeful? What is my greatest hope?

Thursday: Willingness

How much time and energy do we spend walking over the same ground, attempting to prove what we know and find comfort in predictability? To welcome God's guidance and live in harmony with Spirit, we must be open to what we do not know. This receptivity requires the willingness to venture beyond what is comfortable and familiar as we let truth guide us.

Mother Teresa's prayer to live her life as "a pencil in the hand of God" says it powerfully. *Let my life be full. Let it be guided by something more significant than the narrow reaches of self-interest and ego. I am willing to be a divine instrument, surrendering to what is required of me.*

There are several accounts in the Advent story of individuals surrendering to divine will. The themes of their stories are the same, but their particular experiences differ. A significant change in circumstances occurs; intuition perceives a call to embrace that change and discover a divine promise of fulfillment. Whether it is Mary, Joseph, the shepherds, or kings—first, there is fear and wonder. Why is it happening? And why is it happening to *me?* Sometimes life takes a turn into unchartered territory, and we are stunned by what we experience. Why? We ask. Can this be divine will for my life? What good can come from this? Do I have what I need to take the next step?

Where can we find security and well-being in times of uncertainty and immense change? Mary's response to the angel Gabriel who announces the coming birth, says it all: *Behold the handmaid of the Lord. Let it be unto me according to thy word.* First, she is afraid. Then she wonders. After that comes willingness. Her willingness demonstrates the peace found when we *surrender into God.* Notice the word "into." It would still be accurate to say that Mary surrenders "to" God. But "into" conveys something more.

When we become entirely open to follow divine will, we let go of the illusion that we are separate from God. We affirm and know that the word of God, the creative power of God, is already expressing in our life. This affirmation brings a sense of security and complete well-being. God is right where we are, and all must ever be well with us. Through willingness, we surrender *into* divine support.

Practice:

Read over the Christmas story accounts in the New Testament (Matthew Ch. 1 and Luke Ch. 1) and notice how often something surprising, unexpected, or even unwelcome occurs.

The divine mystery touches every life in the story. Each one must grow in faith and willingness to become aware of God's guiding presence. Perhaps we can think of faith as the steps we take (small or large) into the darkness of the unknown with a willingness to believe in the inner light that will illuminate our next step.

Contemplate:

For with God nothing shall be impossible...
And Mary said, let it be unto me according to thy word. —Luke 1:37-38

Free from desire, you realize the mystery.
Caught in desire, you see only the manifestations.
Yet mystery and manifestations
arise from the same source.
This source is called darkness.
Darkness within darkness.
The gateway to all understanding.
—Tao Te Ching, v. 1, Stephen Mitchell, trans.

Reflect:

Think of willingness as complete openness to receive divine support. There are times that we face challenges in life that we do not know how to meet. Willingness is a powerful ally in these situations. We start by doing what we are inspired to do and what we can do. We go as far as we can to meet the challenge. Then we wait. We wait for divine grace to reveal our next step. That grace will provide for us what we could not do for ourselves.

Ask: Am I willing to awaken spiritually and be free?
Am I ready to live in harmony with divine will?

Friday: Sacred Time

Advent coincides with the winter solstice in the Northern Hemisphere, and the summer solstice in the Southern Hemisphere. This transitional period is noted in myths from many times and cultures, which provide an entry into sacred time. Sacred time is a portal. It can take us into the profound, spiritual significance of the time of year, the time in our world, in our lives, and our consciousness.

The Hopi in the Southwest observe Winter Solstice each year as Soyal or Soyalangwul, which means *"Establishing Life Anew for All the World."* Traditionally the first part of the ritual begins underground with cleansing and preparation for recreating the world and the celebration to follow. It's inspiring to consider that the new life we seek is not just our own but a new beginning for the entire world. Often when we approach the end of a year, we are weary of the old and ready for something fresh. Yet, we may neglect to consider the inner work required to make life authentically new.

In modern life, many have lost contact with the 'sacred time' dimension of the holidays. There is often an attempt to celebrate something momentous at Christmas without the essential inner journey that precedes it. Authentic celebrations are organic—they are in harmony with the times, with nature, with God, with our soul. And as an organic process, true celebration tends to unfold from within and move through a natural cycle.

To authentically celebrate the return of light, we must first be open to the darkness—willing to enter into the mystery of sacred time and embrace the possibility of leaving the old behind to create life anew.

Engage in a simple, prayerful ritual such as lighting a candle, washing your hands and feet in preparation for meditation, or chanting a prayer. When you engage in the practice, understand that the purpose of the spiritual ritual is to provide an "entryway" to the liminal, the numinous, spiritual consciousness beyond the ordinary mind. Bring your heart and mind to the action. Feel that you are lifting your consciousness to abide in the awareness of the presence of God.

Practice:

In one of Rumi's poems, he speaks about the practice of True Ablutions and advises us to be aware that such action is not just a matter of physically washing our hands and feet. Instead, we recognize that the ritual of washing hands and feet before prayer and meditation gives us time to turn our awareness away from the world and toward God. With the simple act of washing, we cross the liminal threshold. Rumi offers the prayer for ablution: *Time to say within your heart, I am now going to establish a connection with God.* Whatever ritual you choose, do it to establish that connection.

Contemplate:

No heaven can come to us unless our hearts find rest in today.
Take Heaven!
No peace lies in the future which is not hidden in this present little instant.
Take Peace!
The gloom of the world is but a shadow.
Behind it yet within our reach is Joy.
There is radiance and glory in the darkness,
could we but see — and to see we have only to look.
I beseech you to look.
—Fra Giovanni, excerpt from a letter written in 1513

Reflect:

What is the life I would create anew for all the world? Am I willing to enter sacred time in this season? How do I begin today?

Saturday: Opening to Divine Guidance

And it came to pass, as the angels were gone away from them into heaven, the shepherds said one to another, Let us now go even unto Bethlehem, and see this thing which is come to pass, which the Lord has made known to us. —Luke 2:15

The shepherds of the Christmas story personify intuitive feeling and the quality of humility that allows us to be receptive to divine guidance. Our consciousness, our body, mind, spirit, and heart—the totality of our being—is the dwelling place of God. We will find the divine guidance we need in the realm of our own Self, our conscious awareness. The shepherds watch, wait, and perceive divine inspiration. Then they follow it. Let's go!

At times we may paradoxically yearn for this guidance and ignore its presence or instruction. When the voice of fear drowns out the voice of love, we find it difficult to do what we know in our heart is right for us. Why do we sometimes ignore or fear divine guidance? Perhaps we are afraid that what God will require of us is not what we want for ourselves. At such times, we can ask ourselves who or what is wanting? And why? Could it be that a grander possibility awaits?

When we choose to invite God to direct our life, we must also become willing to follow that guidance. We must keep surrendering the illusional sense that we are separate from the Source. Then we are no longer at odds with our Higher Power but can recognize that divine will for us is what we, ourselves, genuinely desire. Why? Because God is our life, there is no other.

Practice:

Throughout the day, use a mantra, or prayer words, to anchor your attention and awareness in the one Reality expressing as all that is. A simple phrase such as "not two" or "only God" can suffice to erode the tendency to think of our life and God's life as something separate.

There are many moments throughout the day when soul consciousness rises, and awareness lifts into a new way of seeing and being. We can cooperate with this natural tendency by engaging in this practice that restores awareness of our innate wholeness. Use the mantra to affirm truth. Breathe in, "only God." Breathe out, "not two." You can substitute any name for God that is pleasing to you.

Contemplate:

I am always with all beings;
I abandon no one. And
however great your inner darkness,
you are never separate from Me.
Let your thoughts flow past you, calmly;
Keep Me near, at every moment;
Trust Me with your life, because I
am you, more than you yourself are.
—words of Krishna to Arjuna, Bhagavad Gita 9.29-34

Reflect:

Am I willing to fully receive inner guidance by acting upon it?
Can I take one step without knowing everything about where it will lead?
Can I stay open, knowing that insight will come one step at a time?

WHERE DIVINE LOVE ENTERS

ENTERS
WEEK TWO

The power of love is greater than
all of our imperfections.
It will prevail over all our difficulties
and crown our vulnerabilities.

Second Sunday: Where Divine Love Enters

And she brought forth her firstborn son, and wrapped him in swaddling clothes, and laid him in a manger; because there was no room for them at the inn. —Luke 2:7

Great inspiration from the Christmas story is that against all odds, the miracle of the birth occurs. Despite the implausibility of its beginning, despite the misgivings and frailties of the human beings involved, despite the harried circumstances, the miraculous birth occurs, and the Christ child reveals divine love. A child whose very being declares: God is with us! Emmanuel. This birth signifies the awakened spiritual consciousness that knows, that realizes God is with us; God is our life. The advent of Christ Consciousness is the revelation of conscious oneness.

It is fitting that this divine birth occurs in the most humble place. Humility naturally fosters openness to divine grace and its healing power. When we have done all we can and remain open to divine power beyond our efforts, and that power comes, it heals us. The experience transforms us. We can then declare based on our personal experience: God is with us. We know that only God could accomplish such a thing. Such healings forever transform our consciousness.

Divine love finds its way into our lives in the places where we are open and vulnerable, not where we have pride or resistance. At times, the part of our life or ourselves we reject, which is most in need of healing, becomes a likely place for love to enter.

The Christmas story reminds us that the power of love is greater than all of our imperfections. That power will prevail over all our difficulties and crown our vulnerabilities. Imagine a child leading the way! Be encouraged to trust and be open to what can occur through grace, God's supportive influence at work in our lives and our world.

Practice:

The Christmas story provides us with powerful teachings and inspiration about the presence of God moving through the world, unstopped by any obstacle. Metaphysically, "no room at the inn" symbolizes a restless mind, too full of thought activity to perceive the inner Christ. There is no space for divine revelation—no room for awareness of the divine Self.

Make room for the revelation of divine presence in your mind and your life by meditating. Sit quietly in a comfortable, upright position. Close your eyes, and draw your attention within. Notice your breathing. Feel your natural inhalation and exhalation. This will calm the mind. Intend to experience your essential spiritual nature beyond words and thoughts, beyond all limits and conditions. Let your restless thoughts settle. Allow the soul's peace to arise and the inner light of truth to be born in you.

Contemplate:

Effortlessly,
Love flows from God
into all people,
like a bird
who rivers the air
without moving her wings.
—Mechthild of Magdeburg

Reflect:

Grace is divine support that is unmerited, freely provided for all. There are times we experience it and times we remain unaware of it. Yet, we live by grace.

Ask: Can I become more receptive to divine grace? How can I welcome divine love today? Will I?

Monday: A New Government

*For unto us a child is born, unto us a son is given: and the government
shall be upon his shoulder: and his name shall be called Wonderful,
Counselor, The mighty God, The everlasting Father, The Prince of Peace.
Of the increase of his government and peace there shall be no end...*
—Isaiah 9:6-7

The scriptures tell an ancient, ever-new story—people look for a new
ruler, a government change that will usher in peace and plenty. Many
who awaited the Messiah in Jesus' time were hoping for someone to
govern with wisdom and bring about justice and prosperity. This story
repeats itself throughout history, and we see it in our own time.

Some yearn for a new way of life and place their hopes upon a person
believing that once that "right" person is in power, life will improve.
That person will take care of it. There is always a potential for positive
change with new leadership, and we should do our part as conscientious
citizens to make sure we elect and support wise leaders. However, there
are different levels to observe and participate in—physical, mental, and
spiritual. We operate on and are responsible for all levels. Besides
attending to the physical plane of right activity as citizens, we must
consider how leadership reflects a nation or group's collective
consciousness on the mental and spiritual levels. We also examine our
beliefs about the ultimate "savior"—the source of salvation or well-
being. Looking outside ourselves for salvation is an old story of mistaken
understanding, confusion about the real Source. Jesus, himself, tried to
correct this error by pointing out that the kingdom is within.

The *lasting* change we seek must occur in consciousness, in the kingdom
within. When there is an inner change, outer conditions reflect it—both
personally and collectively. The metaphysical adjustment in
government that is transformative is the realization that unseats the
ego from its role as ruler. This change occurs with the revelation of the
Christ Consciousness within. When the Christ light illumines our minds,
there is no end to the peace we experience. The peace of God within us is
unconditional. It isn't ours when something happens or is resolved,
when this goes away, or that comes to us—it is unchanging, always
available. Nothing can take that peace from us; it is without end.

Practice:

Notice who or what occupies the court of your mind and the throne of your heart. Who or what do you turn to as the source of your happiness, peace, or security?

We sometimes spend precious time and energy, entertaining various strategies to try to get what we need. A useful spiritual practice is to "pray our way through" all of that worry and wanting. Pray in God until you have fully expressed what is on your mind and in your heart. Don't hold anything back. Then, wait. Sit in the silence. Be receptive to the arising of peace within you that was previously obscured by your restless thoughts.

Throughout the day, whenever you notice any anxious, worried, or fearful thoughts arising, use that awareness as an opportunity to invite God to take the lead, *to govern in all of your affairs*. Take a moment to be quiet. Recognize that you have turned to God. Relax. In the climate of peace that arises, be receptive to guidance.

Contemplate:

Place your burden at the feet of the Lord of the Universe
who accomplishes everything.
Remain all the time steadfast in the heart,
in the Transcendental Absolute.
God knows the past, present, and future.
God will determine the future for you and accomplish the work.
What is to be done will be done at the proper time. Don't worry.
Abide in the heart and surrender your acts to the divine.
—Sri Ramana Maharshi

Reflect:

Am I willing to release my worries and concerns and invite God to lead?

Tuesday: Embody Truth

I cannot think of a more fitting image to portray the transformation that comes with spiritual awakening than birth—the divine revealing Itself in and through a human body. If we imagine that all the elements of the Christmas story signify some part of us, a stable as the setting for the birth is significant. What are we to make of the stable where the birth takes place?

To discover more about this birthplace, take a few contemplative moments to imagine it. What is a barn or a stable like? Some of the impressions are: fecund, damp, warm, smelly, full of the energy and sounds of animals, humble. There is a lot in common with the human body. Many religions point to the body as the dwelling place of God. Yet many of us either ignore, abuse, or indulge the body, not respecting it as the temple of Spirit.

Ayurveda, yoga's sister science for healthy living, points out three common ways we lose our balance and compromise our health. The first mistake is not honoring time—including the time of day, the season of the year, and period of life. For example, if we stay up too late working or playing on the computer, we are likely to oversleep and feel out of sorts the next day. The season of Advent has the energy of inwardness. If we try to go against the nature of the season by neglecting contemplation and filling our lives with distracting activity, we court a feeling of emptiness deep down.

The second error is the misuse of the senses—either overuse and stimulation or neglect. Listening to too much loud music on headphones or letting our sensual experiences of smell and taste take us beyond the reasonable limits of our digestive capacity are examples of ways we lose our balance through misuse of the senses. The third way we compromise our well-being is by acting against wisdom. It is not listening to our discernment—doing what we know is not useful or neglecting what we know is helpful.

The body is the temple of Spirit. The Lord of Love dwells in every heart. Advent invites us to reflect on our relationship with the body temple. Think about the time, the appropriate use of sense organs, and doing what you know will care for the body temple every day.

Practice:

Be mindful of the three common errors that dishonor the body temple. Remember, they are common, so you are likely to spot them. When you do, use that moment for course correction.

Include the physical body in your sadhana—whether it is hatha yoga, tai chi, Qigong, massage, or going for a walk in nature.

Use your breath to enter the body temple and connect to prana, subtle energy. Feel the life force of your body and know it is alive with Spirit.

Contemplation:

Who is wise,
The eloquent or the quiet person?
Be quiet, and loving and fearless.
For the mind talks.
But the body knows.
—Saying of the Buddha from the Dhammapada, Thomas Byrom, trans.

Reflect:

How do I relate to my physical body? Do I honor and respect it as the temple of God? Is there a simple step toward caring for my body for me to take today?

Wednesday: Journey

One of the paradoxes of spiritual awakening is that it is often spoken of and represented as a journey. People rightfully ask: Why a journey? Why must we travel to arrive at a destination we never left to discover that which was always so? Yet, a journey is indeed a fitting description. While there is no physical journey required, we must make a passage in consciousness—from the darkness of ignorance to the light of truth.

We journey to a higher state of conscious awareness, from being falsely identified with the body and mind to realizing our true nature as eternal Spirit. This pathway of awakening is universal and is the trajectory of everyone's life. We are all on this journey, whether we recognize it or not. It is the inevitable destiny of every person to realize the truth. Because our lives are inseparable from the life of God, what we truly are will be revealed. What is true does not remain hidden.

Patanjali's Yoga Sutras state that life's purpose in this material creation is to experience it and find freedom from it. We are here to experience, enjoy, and find liberation while in the world. We can come to see all that we do in light of life's highest goal of Self- and God-realization. That inner work of the soul is always attempting to rise to the surface of our awareness. There are clues everywhere! The activity of divine grace beckons us to awaken to the sacred nature of life.

Mary and Joseph are required to journey to the city of Bethlehem during the tax season to pay their taxes. It seems that the reason for the journey is a mundane one. The failure to recognize the sacred nature of their travel brings to mind the observation: *Life is what happens while we are busy making other plans.* We engage in outer responsibilities, sometimes imagining that is all there is, yet within us, the inner journey continues in the sanctuary of our soul. This lack of awareness is significant for us to recognize. Always, regardless of what is occurring outwardly, the inner journey of Self- and God-realization is unfolding. When we realize this, we can stay attuned to divine guidance. The outer and inner journeys become one.

Practice:

Whatever you are doing today, recognize that the real "journey" you take is in God. Wherever you go and whatever you do is in, and with, divine support. Remember that the deeper purpose is Self-realization. Let that awareness infuse all that you do.

Use a prayer phrase to capture your attention, such as: "I am working in Spirit." "I am serving in God." "I am walking in God." "I am resting in Spirit."

Contemplate:

Rise up nimbly and go on your strange journey to the ocean of meanings. The stream knows it can't stay on the mountain. —Rumi

And so it was that while they were there, the days were accomplished that she should be delivered. —Luke 2:6

Lead us from the unreal to the Real;
Lead us from the darkness of ignorance to the light of truth;
Lead us from death to immortality.
—Brihadaranyaka Upanishad

Reflect:

How can I bring more awareness to the inner journey as I move through the activity of my days?

Inquire whether your choices are supportive of your life journey of freedom. Will they support liberation or lead to unnecessary complications or bondage to things or situations?

Thursday: Silence

Those who practice meditation soon learn that silence is much greater than not speaking words or the absence of sound. Once our attention and awareness moves beyond the spoken word and then beyond the subtle inner noise of sensation, thought, and feeling and comes to rest in the center of our being, it is there that we discover true silence. We realize silence as empty of words, sound, or image, *but full of presence.* Silence emanates from, and as, the existence of God within us.

Deep silence, beyond words and thoughts, ushers us into the experience of oneness. The Sanskrit word for oneness or unity—*samadhi*—means "holding together" or "to bring together completely." It refers to our ability to bring our attention and awareness to rest in our essential nature as silent, eternal, unchanging, and pure existence-being. It means to be restored to wholeness, returning our conscious awareness to its origin.

Several images from scripture, songs, and prayers of this season point to silence as the fertile ground from which Christ Consciousness can be realized or born. The divine presence is revealed on a "silent night," a "holy night." The shepherds are watching their flocks in the stillness of the night when a divine revelation comes to them.

The first few verses of the Yoga Sutras of Patanjali offer instruction for the experience of silence that allows higher consciousness to be revealed to us and experienced by us. It tells us that samadhi occurs naturally when the mental field is silent—when the restless thought activity has subsided. No longer obscured by the modifications in the mental field, the true Self is revealed. Silent night, holy night! In silence, in wholeness, the true Self is known.

Practice:

When you meditate, intend to meditate superconsciously, to have your awareness restored to its original wholeness. The word "super" means "above or beyond." To meditate superconsciously is to access a higher state of consciousness, beyond our ordinary fragmented state of awareness. The key is to know that superconsciousness is natural to you. When we meditate, we are merely arranging conditions so that awareness can rest in the unchanging silence of pure being.

Beginning meditation with a firm intention to enter the silence of superconsciousness helps avoid the error of being too passive and letting the mind wander. Initially, use a technique such as observing the breath, or a mantra, to focus your attention on a single point. One-pointed concentration will quiet mental restlessness. As soon as you become aware of inner peace or silence, let go of the technique and let your awareness expand into the unbounded silence of your soul.

Contemplate:

In the heart
is a well, filled
with the sound
of silence.
Drink
from it.
One
taste
changes
everything.
How do I know?
The day I stopped
sitting on the edge
and fell in,
told me this.
—Ellen Grace O'Brian, *The Moon Reminded Me*

Reflect:

Silence is a quality of being that permeates the body and the mind. Let us ask ourselves: How silent am I? Do I welcome silence or try to drown it out? What does silence hold for me?

Friday: Divine Ideas

Divine ideas or inspiration usually come to us unbidden. These ideas are often intuitive perceptions that arise when our minds are quiet, and we are receptive. We recognize them as inspiration, glimpses of higher guidance. Sometimes they are simple urgings to act in the moment—call a friend or open a book. Other times, they can be life-changing directives. The nudge comes to change a job, respond to an uncomfortable physical symptom, pursue a path, end a significant relationship. Like Mary in the gospel story, we might ask: *What is this? How can this be? Why me? Why now?*

In the Advent stories, angels deliver these intuitive perceptions or divine ideas. An angel represents our intuitive faculty of soul-knowing. Through our intuition, we can know, discern, and experience insights directly, rather than through our thought process. Intuition comes to us without the mediation of discursive thought.

Intuition arises holistically; it comes in fullness, which allows us to recognize it as accurate. We receive it with a felt sense that is familiar. *We know that we know.* Then we must find a way for that divine idea to take hold and express. The moment that follows the revelation is crucial. How is it received? The thinking aspect of the mind may enter and plant seeds of doubt. *This idea doesn't make sense*, it might say. *How would you ever accomplish such a thing? This plan isn't realistic.* And on it goes. If we follow the lead only of the thinking mind at this juncture, we will abandon the inspiration. Perhaps you have done that at some time. Many of us have disregarded our intuitive insight regretfully to comprehend later how it should or could have been. *I knew it!* We declare. We had the inspiration but not sufficient faith to trust it.

We don't have to discard reason to trust our intuition. Both ways of knowing are essential and come into use at the right time. After we honor our intuition, receive it, and begin to move toward its guidance, our discernment skills can come in as support. Welcoming "the angels of insight" gets better with faith in the One and with practice.

Practice:

Be open to intuitive insight in great and small ways. As you cultivate more profound silence and receptivity through your meditation practice, you will notice that you have more access to intuition.

Expect that divine guidance, through your faculty of intuition, will arise. When it does, receive it. Take some time to be with it, "pondering it in your heart," as the scriptures tell us Mary did. This first phase is just being with it, allowing it to be heard, received, and felt. Then you can inwardly ask if there is anything for you to do to honor this insight with action. Sometimes the response is simply to wait with knowing and let it unfold; other times, there is a first step to take.

Contemplate:

And Mary said, Behold the handmaid of the Lord; be it unto me according to they word. And the angel departed from her.
—Luke 1:38

The mystic intuitively senses Reality and instinctively knows the Truth... Intuition is God in man, revealing to him the Realities of Being.
—Ernest Holmes

Reflect:

Recall the times when you trusted your intuition and the times when you did not. What was your experience?

Ask: What, if anything, prevents me from Self trust?
How can I develop greater confidence in my Self?

Saturday: Expect Revelation

Scriptures of the world's religions may be viewed from various perspectives and yield different insights depending on the approach. We can apply the teachings in scripture to three levels of our being— physical, mental, and spiritual. We can study scripture in its literal and historical context and explore its metaphoric and metaphysical potentials as well.

The physical level of scripture relates to its historical context and literal meaning. It includes the time in history that it was written and what the context was at the time for those teachings. What happened, who wrote or recorded it, what was the writer's purpose, who was the intended reader, and what did the words or actions signify in that period?

The mental level includes psychological and moral teachings. At this level, we find instruction for living an ethical and purposeful life according to spiritual principles taught in a particular tradition. This level is open to exploring image and metaphor, where one can enter into more subtle teachings about the nature of mind and spirit.

The spiritual level conveys insight about spiritual principles and knowledge that is beyond word and thought. Study at this level requires us to contemplate, imagine, and to enter the teaching experientially. At this level, scripture acts as a catalyst to open us to our innate wisdom.

One of the secrets of receiving insight through scripture study is expecting that wisdom will be revealed from within you. Spiritual truth is always eternal, never sectarian, or new. We know the truth when we encounter it and can readily discern that which is false.

Scripture can provide an experience that connects us to the truth within us. Sometimes a good passage for this purpose will be one that we do not readily understand. This "not knowing" provides a space where more profound wisdom can arise. Be curious about the meaning and pray for revelation or insight. Expect that it will come. All knowledge of God and God's creative processes indwells you at the soul level of your being. Revelation is the unfolding of innate soul knowledge.

Practice:

Read some passages of the scripture of your choice. During this Advent journey, you might read accounts of the birth of Jesus in the gospels of Matthew or Luke, or prophecies of the coming Messiah in the Hebrew Bible, Isaiah, Chapters 9 & 11. Identify the scripture's physical, mental, and spiritual levels. When you come to something that interests you, but you do not fully understand, write about it. First, write what you think it means. Then write your questions about it, and identify what puzzles you.

After your meditation, when your mind is quiet, contemplate the scripture you read. Examine your felt sense of it—what do you notice as you reflect on it? Expect insight to be revealed. It may come to you at that moment. Or, as more frequently happens, it will surface at another time as clear understanding, like a puzzle piece falling into place.

Contemplate:

A lifetime is not enough to know all the scriptures. Therefore, realize the essence of the scriptures. —Lahiri Mahasaya

And those who err in spirit will come to understanding. —Isaiah 29:24

Do you have the patience to wait until your mud settles and the water is clear? —Lao Tzu

Reflect:

Can I approach scripture with an open heart and mind? Am I willing to allow its spiritual meaning to be revealed to me?

NEW IDENTITY
WEEK THREE

Bliss is the joy of Self-knowing,
recognizing the light of God
that reveals our spiritual nature.

Third Sunday: Our Divine Identity

And the angel came in unto her, and said, "Hail, thou that art highly favored..." —Luke 2:28

When the angel Gabriel appears to Mary to announce the coming birth of the Christ child, he does not address her by her given name. He doesn't greet her as Mary but calls her "One Who Is Highly Favored" and "One Who Is Blessed Among Women." It is a provocative greeting, and it causes Mary to wonder. *What kind of greeting is that*, she says. She finds it curious and unsettling. As we explore this scene's metaphysical meaning, we see that she is being called to a new identity. Her consciousness is transforming, and with that, her old identity.

When the revelation comes to her, it raises her from old ideas and attachments. There is an immediate impact. We can note that she does not receive this revelation at the level of ego or personal identity. Her response is consistent with an opening to soul-knowing, with surrendered devotion to God. Imagine an inspiration that comes and says, "You Are Great! Most Highly Favored! God is with you." If such an inspiration were to be received by the ego, the false self, it would be tempting to feel proud, and perhaps, even to boast about having a spiritual experience. However, Mary's story is instructive of what occurs when the soul is utterly receptive to the word, or the creative power, of God. She, too, finds another name for herself, saying, "Behold the handmaid of the Lord."

This naming in the story, both from the angel and Mary, indicates her identity transformation. Before spiritual awakening, we tend to identify ourselves with our bodies, minds, roles, successes, or failures. When we remove our awareness from involvement and identification with those mental patterns, it comes to rest in our essential nature—which is divine. We experience That which we essentially are—pure existence-being. We discover our true Self. One with the One, a new identity is ours.

Practice:

Pay attention to the ways you "name" yourself (and others) throughout the day. What kind of adjectives come to mind in moments of self-awareness? So often, the names we inwardly utter are not consistent with our highest nature but our lowest—"O Absent-Minded One!" or "You Who Lack Awareness."

Cultivate your divine identity by refusing to name yourself in ways that pull you down. If you notice any self-commentary that is not uplifting, change it by taking a moment to consider your real identity.

Contemplate:

At each stage of progressive awakening to authentic Self- and God-knowledge, the devotee's new state of awareness must be harmoniously integrated with the mind, personality, and body. This process is most effectively accomplished by appropriate, conscious living every moment of each day. —Roy Eugene Davis

Is it not written in your law, I said, Ye are gods? —teachings of Jesus, John 10:34

Tat Tvam Asi. That Thou Art. —Vedic Mahavakya

Reflect:

Who do I think I am? Who do I tell myself I am?
What do I call others? What does that say about me?

Monday: Nurturing Insight in Silence

And you will have joy and gladness. —Luke 1:14

Several of the scripture stories surrounding the birth of Christ Consciousness include themes of watching, waiting and being self-contained. The story of Zacharias, the husband of Elizabeth and temple priest, who is visited by the angel Gabriel, is one example. Viewed metaphysically, this story is about how divine insight is revealed to us when we are open to it and can wait in the silence for it to unfold.

The visitation of angels can be interpreted as divine ideas arising in the mental field. Gabriel represents conscious awareness of our spiritual identity and the infinite potential within us. When Gabriel visits Zacharias to announce that he and his aged wife Elizabeth will give birth to a child, Zacharias questions: *how shall I know this?* This vision does not correspond with facts. It is not logical. Have you ever had a glimpse of divine possibility? Seen or been inspired to something beyond what you had ever considered possible? Perhaps like Zacharias, you may have thought, "how can I trust this inspiration?" "It doesn't make sense." When this occurs, what do we do? Do we embrace the inspiration? Dismiss it? Or give it time and space to unfold?

When Zacharias expresses his doubt, Gabriel tells him that he will be struck mute, unable to speak about this revelation until it comes to pass. Taken literally, it might sound like punishment. Understood metaphysically, it signifies that spiritual inspiration is received in silence beyond words and thoughts and cannot be spoken.

When Zacharias leaves the temple after Gabriel's visitation, he meets people waiting outside who wonder why he took so long. This "crowd of people" represents the ordinary thinking mind that can become restless after we've been meditating for a while. Zacharias cannot tell them what has occurred because the consciousness level of the sense mind cannot comprehend an experience beyond words and thoughts. When we see into the heart of the story, we find the encouragement to allow spiritual insight to be nurtured in the silence of the soul, avoiding the temptation to too quickly take it into the realm of thought and reason. If we can let it be, we often find that greater clarity comes with guidance for the right action.

Practice:

The time spent in superconscious meditation can contribute to new insight, inspiration, and creative energy. After resting in our essential spiritual nature beyond ordinary thought activity for some time, we may notice insights arising. It can be tempting to abandon meditation and instead spend that time thinking about these new ideas. However, welcoming thoughts into the temple of meditation (no matter how creative they are) can quickly become a habit that will undermine the ability to meditate deeply. Time spent in meditation is the occasion to trust that we can let go of grasping or working on anything and simply be present. Trust that any authentically divine inspiration that arises will remain with you when you finish meditating.

Contemplate:

In the temple of silence, in the temple of peace, I will meet Thee, I will touch Thee, I will love Thee, and coax Thee to my altar of peace.
—chant by Paramahansa Yogananda

The best things cannot be told. —Heinrich Zimmer

Reflect:

Am I willing to let inspiration unfold? How do I nurture insights that come to me?

Tuesday: Letting Go

And it came to pass, as the angels were gone away from them into heaven, the shepherds said to one another, Let us now go. —Luke 2:15

Many of the Advent stories involve leaving home and venturing forth to meet the unknown. The change of seasons before us reflects the call to inner transformation. In the Western Hemisphere, the muted landscape of late autumn is incredibly beautiful. The stark contrast of the last deep colored leaves that remain on the deciduous trees against the dark grey skies announces: change is coming! With the support of the cold and the wind, the few remaining leaves drift, twirl, and dive toward earth. This exquisite dance of letting go is a prelude to the stillness of winter. The bare trees will work in silence, gather inner sustenance, and burst forth with wild green in the spring. But the letting go must come first.

I suspect most of us could learn this simple lesson from nature: *letting go is essential.* For us, it must happen on many levels—physical, mental, emotional, and spiritual. We let go of things we no longer use, need, or appreciate, let go of outdated or mistaken ideas, let go of our attachments to particular outcomes, and even release relationships when the connection is no longer present. The most profound release is freeing ourselves from identification with the false self. The Buddha said, "You are as the yellow leaf...What will you take with you?"

The world of nature, which includes our bodies and our minds, continually changes. Only our essential, spiritual nature remains. After the yellow leaf metaphor, the Buddha concluded, "All things arise and pass away. But the awakened awake forever." Letting go of the familiar and venturing forth into the unknown is paradoxically preparation for meeting that which has always been and ever will be.

Practice:

Contemplate the way change occurs in nature and your life. How do you relate to change? Are you able to welcome it?

Meditate until you experience that which does not change, the ground of being. How does the experience of changelessness affect our ability to move through life's seasons and changes?

Contemplate:

God works without instrument and without image. And the freer you are from images the more receptive you are to [God's] interior operation... the closer you are to it. All things must be forsaken. —Meister Eckhart

God, give us grace to accept with serenity the things that cannot be changed, courage to change the things that should be changed, and the wisdom to distinguish the one from the other. —Reinhold Niebuhr

Reflect:

Am I trying to hold on to something that is ready to change? Am I willing to let go? What does letting go require of me?

Wednesday: Rise Up

Rise up nimbly and go on your strange journey to the ocean of meanings. The stream knows it can't stay on the mountain. —Rumi

Mary's response to the angel Gabriel is sometimes seen as a passive "let it be," an opening to divine will without choice or deliberation. Yet, there are clues in the story that reveal her active participation that we can recognize as intentional surrendered devotion. First, she questions the angel's greeting that she is highly favored and blessed. What could that mean? She listens to the prophecy and questions again. The angel tells her that what happens will be beyond her, "the power of the Highest will overshadow you." Then he reveals that her elderly cousin Elizabeth has also conceived. After hearing these three announcements, after questioning and contemplating them, she responds: "Behold the handmaid of the Lord; let it be unto me according to thy word."

What Mary does immediately after receiving this inspiration is indicative of faith—she acts on it. She quickly goes to visit her cousin Elizabeth. She's inspired and moved to act. She ventures out with this new understanding—moving into the world to meet her destiny as an active participant in it.

Mary didn't know what would occur when she met with Elizabeth, but she goes with faith grounded in her inner experience. Her choice to visit Elizabeth reveals and magnifies the awareness of the activity of divine grace in both of their lives. What inspiration can we draw from this part of the story? As Rumi says, "*the stream knows it cannot stay on the mountain.*" Spiritual inspiration must be received, realized, and expressed. When we are given a divine inspiration and take a step toward its expression, more is revealed to us, often astounding us with its expansive nature.

Practice:

Flex your "inspiration muscles" by acting on insights you recognize are in harmony with the highest good. Sometimes it is the inspiration to offer a kind word, give a gift of support or service, or enter the temple of silent meditation.

Many times, we are prone to ignore such inspiration. We recognize it as good but tell ourselves we will get to it later. We then discover that "later" has passed, and we have not acted upon the good that inspired us. Then the inspiration and energy pass, and we are left with a sense of regret or missed opportunity.

Don't let the opportunity for a blessing pass you by. Decide to act on at least one inspiration.

Contemplate:

Be quick to do good.
If you are slow,
The mind, delighting in mischief,
Will catch you...
Set your heart on doing good.
Do it over and over again,
And you will be filled with joy.
—sayings of the Buddha, the Dhammapada, Thomas Byrom, trans.

Reflect:

What am I inspired to do?

Thursday: The Inner Tree

All my thoughts are decorating the Christmas tree of meditation with the rare gifts of devotion, sealed with golden heart-prayers that Christ may come and receive my humble gifts.
—Paramahansa Yogananda

One of the first heralds of Christmastime in our neighborhood is the corner city lots that fill up with evergreen trees overnight. The rows of cut trees seem to invite passersby to take them home, decorate them, and let the festive season begin. Among those who follow a religious, spiritual, or cultural custom of tree trimming, there are many ways to engage in the ritual.

Even if it is not part of your tradition or your personal inclination to put up a tree, the presence of Christmas trees is undeniable in the Advent season—whether in homes, on front lawns, in offices, government buildings, or shops. Many people treasure their annual ritual of finding a tree and decorating it, perhaps in ways that honor long-standing family traditions. Others approach it as a chore, one more thing to do in an already busy time. For those on the path of Self- and God-realization, this ubiquitous tree offers some rich symbolism for deep contemplation.

Beyond the physical activity or tradition of decorating a tree, it can be a rich experience to reflect on its inner meaning. The symbol of the tree has represented many things through the ages—the evergreen of eternal life, the tree of life from the Garden of Eden, the living divine presence among us, or the Christ. Paramahansa Yogananda referred to the "Christmas tree of meditation," which encourages us to consider how it can relate to the inner experience of divine communion. The tree can represent the body with its spinal pathway, the channel for subtle energy to ascend as one awakens to Cosmic Consciousness, signified by the star at its apex. As we reflect on this mystical tree representing our inner life, we can think of the gifts of our pure intentions we would offer to God with love and devotion.

Practice:

After your meditation, set aside a time for visualization and contemplation. Inwardly envision a beautiful Christmas tree with a star shining on its top. Imagine yourself placing gifts of love and devotion around your inner tree. What would you most like to offer? What brings you great joy to give?

Contemplate:

The traditional "Christmas tree" is a very ancient custom which exalts the value of life, as in winter the evergreen becomes a sign of undying life. In general, the tree is decorated and Christmas gifts are placed under it...The message of the Christmas tree, therefore, is that life is "ever green" if one gives: not so much material things, but of oneself: in friendship and sincere affection, and fraternal help and forgiveness, in shared time and reciprocal listening. —Pope John Paul II

Trees do not preach learning and precepts. They preach, undeterred by particulars, the ancient law of life. —Herman Hesse

Reflect:

What do trees give me? How can a tree teach me about this season? What am I called to give?

Friday: Keeping Watch

And there were in the same country shepherds abiding in the field, keeping watch over their flock by night. —Luke 2:8

In that same country, "in that same consciousness," where the Christ is born, the shepherds are keeping watch. We can associate the shepherds with the qualities of mindfulness, meditative awareness, devotion, and concentration. They watch mindfully, paying attention throughout the night. The sheep they tend to are like thoughts that can wander in any direction. The job of the shepherd is to be awake and aware, take notice, and stay focused. The shepherd's task is an apt description of the skills we need to be successful in meditation.

In the "field"—or within the consciousness that has been quieted by concentration—a light appears. This light announces the Christ, the light of God within us. An angel brings a message of peace and great joy —*the Christ, has come!* To view the shepherds' story metaphysically, recognize it as the revelation of Christ that occurs when the mental field is calm and quiet. Seeing the radiant inner light of Christ Consciousness at the spiritual eye is often accompanied by the experience of bliss or great joy. Bliss is the joy of Self-knowing, recognizing the light of God that reveals our spiritual nature.

The Advent teaching to "keep watch" encourages us to bring greater intentionality to our meditation practice in particular and spiritual focus in general. When we focus our attention on a single point during meditation, the restless activity of thought subsides, and the mental field becomes receptive to the revelation of Self-knowing. We can also let the inspiration to "keep watch" remind us that this quality of mindful attention is useful at all times. To watch and wait is to stay open and receptive to divine insight—during meditation or activity.

Practice:

In Patanjali's eight-limbed system for experiencing superconscious meditation, he identifies concentration as an essential precursor to meditation. We concentrate on something that has a soothing effect on the mind, such as observing our breath or mentally repeating a mantra.

When you use a tool for concentration to prepare for meditation, observe its effect on your mental field. As we become more proficient at concentrating on a single point, we can perceive a change in the quality of our attention. The initial stage of concentration requires a degree of effort. Attention wanders, and we must redirect it again and again to our chosen focus. However, once the mental field becomes purified and calm, attention will naturally flow into a meditative state. It is no longer distracted by restlessness.

Watch for the moment when concentration becomes meditation. Then let go of the technique and "abide in the field" of divine consciousness. Be there. Awake. Aware. Watchful.

Contemplate:

The pageantry of Jesus' coming to earth lacked no detail of symbolic significance. As with the shepherds on the hillside, the shepherds of man's faith, devotion, and meditation will be bathed in the light of realization and lead those devotees who are humble in spirit to behold the infinite presence of Christ newborn within them.
—Paramahansa Yogananda

Reflect:

How dedicated am I to meditation? Do I bring the quality of devotion or focused attention to it? How might I enhance my practice?

Saturday: A Fitting Place

And they came with haste, and found Mary, and Joseph, and the babe lying in a manger. —Luke 2:16

Luke's gospel identifies Jesus' birthplace as a lowly stable, where a manger becomes his cradle. This imagery provides us with profound lessons to consider concerning our spiritual journey of Self- and God-realization or awakening to Christ within. The simple humility of the stable is a stark contrast to palaces, the usual birthplace for one who is called a prince or a king. Not a gilded bed but a manger, a simple feeding trough, is the place that receives this child. What inspiration can we draw from this?

Inwardly, the manger represents the place in us that receives the Christ revelation—our mind and consciousness. The "cradle of our consciousness" must be purified if we are to receive the revelation of divine truth. It must be cleansed of pride, self-will, and worldly attachments. Thus, the manger is a fitting symbol. It is lowly, open, and a place of nourishment. Ordinarily, it contains food or water, that which sustains life. Here, we understand nourishment to be the presence of God that maintains and supports all life.

Spiritual teachings in the Yoga tradition point out that we cannot create a spiritual condition. We cannot make ourselves more spiritual, cause the inner Christ to awaken in us, or make Self-realization occur. We cannot do any of that because our essential nature is already spiritual, already a perfect expression of God. The Christ of God is already awake within us. Our spiritual nature is unconditional; it is without cause. Nothing we do can change it. Rightly understood, our spiritual practice is not to create "a spiritual self," but to arrange conditions (both inwardly and outwardly) that allow our essential nature to be realized. We purify the mind through devotion, pranayama, prayer, mantra, and meditation to become a fit receptacle to receive the Christ within.

Practice:

Alternate nostril breathing is a useful tool for regulating the breath and balancing the subtle energy in our system. This practice results in relaxation, mental clarity, emotional calm, and enhanced intuition. Follow these steps:

1. Prepare for meditation with correct posture and interiorizing attention.
2. Position your index and middle fingers of your right hand on your forehead at the spiritual eye. Those two fingers will remain stable during the exercise to anchor your inner gaze at the third eye center. (You will use your thumb to close the right nostril and your ring finger to close the left.)
3. Bring attention to the breath by gently but thoroughly inhaling and exhaling one time through both nostrils.
4. After exhaling, close the right nostril with your right thumb and breathe in through your left nostril.
5. Using your thumb and ring finger, close both nostrils and pause the breath momentarily.
6. Keep the left nostril closed and open the right as you breathe out through the right side.
7. With the left nostril still closed, breathe in through the right side.
8. Once again, close both sides and retain the breath for a moment.
9. Now open the left nostril while keeping the right nostril closed, and breathe out. This alternation makes one complete round. Six rounds is a useful beginning practice.

Do this practice gently and without any strain. Do not hold the breath; only pause slightly where indicated. If you are under a doctor's care, consult your physician before practicing breath regulation.

Contemplate:

I will prepare for the coming of the Omnipresent baby Christ by cleaning the cradle of my consciousness, now rusty with selfishness, indifference, and sense attachments; and by polishing it with deep, daily divine meditation, introspection, and discrimination. —Paramahansa Yogananda

Reflect:

Am I trying to become more spiritual?
Am I willing to accept my divine identity?

AWAKENING IN THIS LIFETIME

WEEK FOUR

The peace that we pray for in our world,
the love we hope for,
the healing we yearn for,
and the joy we welcome
are natural expressions of spiritual awakening.

Fourth Sunday: A Useful Mantra

And when Zacharias saw him, he was troubled, and fear fell upon him.
But the angel said unto him, Fear not. —Luke 1:12, 13

One of the things that happen consistently in several of the Advent stories is that when the angel appears to bring good news—news of the coming of the Christ, the announcement of new life, joy, and peace—the first response is not joy or praise, but fear. In each story, this initial reaction to the divine inspiration is met by the angel's mantra: *Fear not.*

Fear is our usual, instinctual reaction to anything unknown that threatens life as we know it. The Advent story is about a new spiritual identity destined to overturn the ego's control and bring about new life through a fundamental change in consciousness. This transformation is unsettling to the ego. It is not unusual to experience fear or contraction in light of the soul's readiness to express more fully. Sometimes we experience apprehension when we discern the call to live in a new way. Perhaps that call is to speak the truth we have previously withheld, seek work in harmony with our life purpose, or give more generously than before. These new behaviors can trigger the ego's alarm system, which serves as a protective mechanism. Watch out!—it will say when we are about to do a new thing. When we experience this, we can use our discernment to reveal whether fear is useful or not.

Sometimes this contraction of fear is experienced in meditation. Samadhi, or experiences of superconsciousness, require us to let go to expand awareness into our higher Self. When this expansion of consciousness occurs, it can be joyful and yet provoke an ego-based reaction. People say things like, "I was meditating, and I felt so much joy arising, and then I got scared, and my meditation experience stopped." The fear comes from holding onto the body-mind as our primary identity, instead of knowing that we are returning to rest in our true nature as spiritual beings.

Remembering our essential nature as unbounded Supreme Consciousness, knowing that we are spiritual beings expressing through mind and body, can help us step into these expansive experiences. Walking in faith, we can say the powerful mantra: *fear not.*

Practice:

Notice thoughts and feelings arising that are fear-based, especially as they appear concerning new, positive behaviors. Inquire into those thoughts and feelings. Discern what their origin is. Notice what changes as you shift your attention and awareness from identifying with body, mind, and ego and embrace your essential spiritual nature.

Contemplate:

The Blessed Lord spoke: Whence has this timidity of yours come to you in time of danger? Do not become a coward, Arjuna. This is not suitable to you. Abandoning base faintheartedness, Stand up, Arjuna!
—words of Krishna to Arjuna, Bhagavad Gita 2.2-3

Reflect:

When have I noticed fear arising? Does it coincide with expanding my potential? How can I meet the potential fears of this season with the mantra "fear not?"

Monday: A Time for Prayer

...without prayer there is no inward peace. —Mahatma Gandhi

The metaphysical approach to prayer is never about finding help to fix a problem. Instead, prayer is a way to enter divine communion, *where the problem no longer exists.* Through prayer, we relinquish the sense of being a separate self and consciously participate in divine wholeness. In this consciousness, we are not asking for guidance or a solution to our problems. We are not asking God to open doors for us to flee our difficulties. *In mystical prayer, there is no problem to be fixed or difficulty to escape.*

From our human perspective, we rail at this teaching. "Wait a minute! Of course, there is a problem, and I am suffering. How can you say there is no problem? I can see the problem, and the world has a lot of problems and a lot of suffering too!" From this perspective, there is a real problem, and that is why we have come to God in prayer. We need help with our challenges, and we do not want them dismissed as unreal or unimportant. It sounds dangerously like denial to affirm that problems are not real, fly into some spiritual solution, and imagine it will all go away.

Yes, the problem is real, and certainly the suffering is real. The teachings do not deny that, nor do they suggest we try to imagine them away. But here is the key to spiritual understanding: *whatever the problem is, it is a changeable condition.* A human condition brought about by causes is always subject to the laws of change. No situation has any power to sustain itself; it has no *independent* reality. There is only one power and one reality—and that reality and power is God. Only God is all-powerful, eternal, and unchanging.

In prayer, we cease to believe the problem itself is powerful, that it has any power of its own, is fixed or unchanging, or that we can solve it from the level of consciousness that brought it about. We cease believing in two powers, trying to pit one against the other. We realize that God is the only power. In our prayer, we rest in that power. Not denying the problem, but seeing through its insubstantial nature, we come to rest in divine harmony. We discover our innate wholeness. All power, all healing is there.

Practice:

The best time for prayer is after meditation. Thought activity has subsided, and there is a sense of being immersed in Spirit.

Spend some time in prayer after your meditation by inwardly cultivating the awareness that all is in divine order. Feel this to be true. "Pray your way through" any inner conversation about conditions until you consciously abide in wholeness, aware that all will ever be well in God.

Contemplate:

An affirmative prayer:

Beloved God:
Your divine light—life of all the world—shines in the sanctuary of my soul.
Though it has been obscured—clouded over by wrong ideas, thoughts of separation from You, pride and self-will—it is shining still.
It is shining now.
Though Winter is here and the days grow dark,
my soul light is becoming brighter.
I release the past. I free myself from the tyranny of conditions.
They hold no power over me.
I kindle the light of divine remembrance.
I claim my true identity.
I am truly blessed. I am highly favored.
I see all in the light of Truth.
Om Peace Amen.

Reflect:

Am I willing to release my belief in the power of conditions? Can I welcome Spirit as the only power in my life?

Tuesday: Dynamic Balance

The accounts o f the birth of Jesus in the gospels of Luke and Matthew are different. In fact, they are vastly different. What are we to make of this? The account in Matthew tells the story of the visiting kings and the attempted intervention of Herod. Luke makes no mention of that but tells us of the shepherds inspired by a vision who come to adore the child. Luke gives us a perspective of Mary's experience; Matthew focuses on Joseph. If we don't lock ourselves into a purely literal reading of the texts, we can hold these differences together and discover some valuable insights into the inner story. Both stories affirm different qualities within us that are essential to our wholeness.

The story in Luke is primarily focused on feminine qualities. Here we find Mary's experience and her demonstration of the complete receptivity of the soul. In many traditions, the soul—whether of a man or a woman—is seen as feminine due to its receptive nature. The soul is beyond gender. However, to name it feminine is to affirm its primary quality as being receptive to God. God's presence and power give life to the soul, and the soul is receptive to that life. The Gospel of Luke also tells the story of the shepherds. We learn of their humble, earthy, and intuitive qualities—all considered feminine.

In Matthew, the focus is on Joseph. Joseph's first response to learning of the impending birth is to use his mind to figure out the best way to deal with it. He then has a dream, which gives him a revelation beyond thought. The wise men, too, show this rational bent as they inquire, "Where is he that is born king of the Jews?" The intellectual inclination associated with thought is traditionally considered a masculine quality.

When we explore the story by holding the accounts side by side, we can see that the feminine qualities of devotion, surrender, and intuition are essential. So are masculine attributes of reason, discernment, and decisive action. The feminine qualities of devotion and receptivity without clear wisdom can become too sentimental or fail to take action on the inspiration. The masculine quality of reason without surrender and devotion can become too arrogant and self-willed. A balance of feminine receptivity and masculine action is ideal.

Practice:

Reflect on how you experience the balance of your masculine and feminine qualities. Do you tend to be too emotional or passive? Too "heady" or intellectual in your approach? Which quality do you need most right now to bring a healthier balance to your life?

In yoga, the ideal path integrates *bhakti*, the way of devotion, with *jnana*, the wisdom path. Making sure that our *sadhana* or spiritual practice includes prayer and surrender along with study and contemplation is a good step for cultivating balance.

Contemplate:

All things have their backs to the female
and stand facing the male.
When male and female combine,
all things achieve harmony.
—Tao Te Ching, v. 42, Stephen Mitchell, trans.

Reflect:

Am I being invited to cultivate more balance in my life? How would I bring that about?

Wednesday: Spiritual Friendship

When the angel Gabriel announces to Mary the miraculous birth that will come through her, he tells her that her cousin Elizabeth will also experience a miraculous birth. He informs her that her cousin, who is older and was considered infertile, is now in her sixth month of pregnancy. There is hardly a pause in the story between the lines, "And the angel departed from her" and "Mary arose in those days and went into the hill country with haste and entered the house of Zacharias and greeted Elizabeth." Something is happening in their inner lives that draws them together immediately and powerfully. Can you imagine the excitement, energy, inspiration, or curiosity that has Mary move so quickly to visit Elizabeth? She is not disappointed with what she finds. Divine grace permeates their meeting and further expands their joy.

When Mary enters the house and Elizabeth hears her greeting, the baby in Elizabeth's womb leaps. This encounter spiritually inspires Elizabeth. She speaks out to affirm Mary's transformation and the blessed nature of the child within her. In light of this affirmative reception, Mary, too, is inspired to offer praises to God and a magnificent vision for an awakened world.

One of the themes of this part of the story is the significance of spiritual friendship. Through their meeting, both women are inspired, affirmed, and encouraged to trust their most profound inner experiences. In the atmosphere of spiritual recognition, they share their visions.

In spiritual friendship, God's omnipresence is revealed between us and as us. Experiencing the presence of divine grace permeating our relationships strengthens our faith, as it did for Mary and Elizabeth.

Practice:

Appreciate and encourage divine grace in your spiritual friendships by focusing on uplifting conversation supporting a spiritually awakened life. Be committed to uplifting one another through positive conversation, examples of virtuous conduct, and gratitude for the grace that you experience.

Contemplate:

Be with those who help your being. —Rumi

Reflect:

Reflect on how spiritual friendships have been an essential part of your spiritual journey of awakening. How have you been encouraged by others to deepen your faith? How have you been a source of encouragement to others?

Thursday: The True Self

Many years ago, I offered contemplation and meditation retreats during Advent to explore how the season's themes could inspire our inner lives. One of the retreat exercises was to read the stories of the birth of Jesus from Luke and Matthew's gospels and reflect on all of the elements of the story—including the people, places, animals, stars, and angels. The next step was to consider what quality these characters might represent to you. Perhaps the ox has you think about being steadfast or of being "yoked," tied to something that guides your life. The star may bring to mind being inspired by a vision, and so forth.

After learning about the story metaphysically (as a reflection of the psyche), everyone drew a slip of folded paper with the name of a character or component from the story. Their hidden choice might be the donkey, Mary, a shepherd, the manger, or any of the other parts. The person who drew the Christ child and the person who drew Herod often (understandably) had very different experiences. What I found interesting was that year after year, the same thing would occur. The person with the invitation to reflect on the Christ child would find it not only mysterious but challenging to relate to. Yet, time and again, the person drawing Herod would have no trouble recognizing the qualities he represents.

Herod is easily recognizable as the false self, the ego that must control everything to maintain his position. Herod demands to know where and what time the Christ child is born. He says he wants to worship him too. But the wise men see through his cunning and do not return to inform him. Although Herod has an influential role in the story, it is fitting that he is not included in the birth scene. The false self, which insists on being separate from God, cannot remain when the light of the true Self dawns. That true Self is the Christ within you, within all.

Practice:

Reflect on all of the elements of the story of the birth of Christ. Include the animals, stable, the inn, the main, and sub-characters. Notice if any of the parts capture your attention or seem incredibly mysterious to you. Contemplate that component of the story as if it reflects a quality within you. Explore it with your felt sense, your intuitive grasp of its significance at this time in your life.

Contemplate the qualities of Christ, of your divine nature. Make a list of them—love, peace, compassion, generosity, and more. All of these qualities of God exist within us and are meant to be expressed through us.

One of the practices in Patanjali's Yoga Sutra instructs us to purify our hearts and our minds by contemplating the lives and consciousness of spiritually enlightened people who are free from attachment. Contemplate the life of a saint or sage who inspires you. Imagine what it would be like to experience that awakened consciousness. Know that same divine consciousness is within you.

Contemplate:

It is only because of ignorance that the Self appears to be finite. When ignorance is banished, the Self, which does not admit to any multiplicity, reveals itself by itself like the sun when a cloud is removed. —Shankara

When the fluctuations in one's mind and awareness are transcended during meditation and consciousness is purified, the supreme Self is realized. —Lahiri Mahasaya

Reflect:

What am I learning about my inner qualities as I contemplate the symbols of this season? Can I see them as prompts to wholeness?

Am I willing to claim my true identity and take responsibility for cultivating the divine qualities within me?

Friday: Protecting New Life

Joseph's transformation in the Advent story indicates the change that can take place in our understanding when we have a spiritual experience. Joseph's mind is changed; his inner experience transforms it. When confronted with the dilemma of his pregnant fiancé, he uses his mind to try to find a solution. While he is thinking about what to do, he falls asleep and dreams. An angel appears to him in the dream and reveals the spiritual nature of what is occurring. He follows the dream wisdom that inspires him to accept Mary as his wife and welcome this new life.

Joseph's first response to what is occurring is to try to figure it out. But spiritual inspiration cannot be contained or fully understood by the thinking mind. Thus, Joseph has a spiritual experience in a dream—an intuitive insight that expands his ability to embrace this change. There are times when we, too, must look beyond what the mind can comprehend and open ourselves to a more profound insight that will help us move forward with faith.

After the child is born, Joseph has another dream that instructs him to keep the child safe from Herod, who seeks to destroy the child. The awakened faculty of discernment and intuitive wisdom is guided by the higher true Self, not directed by ego. When the mental field is purified and transformed through spiritual realization, it can then serve truth. Joseph represents the mind that becomes purified and generates right, or dharmic, action. When our mental field is clear, and our faculty of discernment is purified, spiritual realization is protected from the ego, from doubts and fears that might obscure or crush it.

Joseph is the protector of new life. He arranges conditions for the well-being of Mary and the baby, keeping them out of Herod's reach. So, it is for our clarified discernment. Soul-inspired wisdom must be protected from the ego's attempts to destroy it. Identifying these components of our psyche helps us nurture new inspiration and give it the time it needs to develop before being unduly exposed to the ego's tendency to take over.

Practice:

To bring more clarity and understanding to a situation in your life, use the example of Joseph. Think about the situation and consider your options, but then open yourself to a direct, intuitive insight that does not depend on logic. When reasoning something through does not satisfy the heart, be willing to wait until your intuition reveals deeper understanding or wisdom. Remember that we all have within us the ability to know the truth and be divinely guided.

With the dawning of your intuitive insight, bring forth the protective capacity of discernment that can create a gestation period, allowing insight the time it needs to develop. Avoid immediately turning it over to the harsh light of ordinary thinking and the motives of the ego.

Contemplate:

The sage is guided by what he feels and not by what he sees.
He lets go of that and chooses this.
—Tao Te Ching, v. 12, Gia-fu Feng and Jane English, trans.

Reflect:

Can I relate to Joseph's story with my own experience of not being able to figure out something significant to me? Am I willing to be curious about the stirrings of my heart? Do I have the patience to wait until clarity arises within me?

Can I trust my intuition and act on it at the appropriate time? What are some ways that I protect "the new life" of my dreams and inspirations?

Christmas Eve: In This Lifetime

The birth of Christ, the revelation of God with us, is an eternally present possibility. God is the eternal life of every person. No one has ever been, or will ever be, separate from the one Reality that is God. The birth awaited on Christmas Eve is realizing this truth, its dawning in our consciousness, and fulfilling its promise in our world. The Christ that is to be born must be realized in the hearts (the essential nature) of people. Since we are all expressions of God, this awakening is our inevitable destiny. Sooner or later, what we indeed are will be known. Why not commit ourselves to this awakening now, in this lifetime?

The most formidable impediment to the dawning of this essential realization is the tendency to cling to a false sense of self. We mistakenly identify ourselves as mortal beings with a soul instead of recognizing that we are souls expressing through a mind and body. Once we understand our true nature as spiritual, then we can open ourselves to experiencing it directly. Knowledge of our true nature and the direct experience of it is realization. This realization is the birth of a new consciousness and a new way of living.

Through the ages, enlightened ones, including Jesus, have proclaimed the truth of our spiritual nature, encouraged us to discover that truth, and live by it. On Christmas Eve, a time when hearts worldwide are turned to God, when the spiritual vibrations of hope and faith permeate the atmosphere, let us kindle the light of our commitment to spiritual awakening.

The peace that we pray for in our world, the love we hope for, the healing we yearn for, and the joy we welcome are natural expressions of spiritual awakening. What the world most needs is this awakening. Let us pray for it today and believe in our hearts it is possible now.

Practice:

Embrace the idea that spiritual enlightenment is your inevitable destiny. Know that you are already enlightened at the core of your being, a pure expression of the one divine life of God. Identify Self- and God-realization as your life's purpose and goal. Consider any changes you want to make to arrange conditions in your life to support that goal. Decide which change should be the first step. Make a plan and begin it today. Walk faithfully towards your goal.

Contemplate:

You are gods; you are all children of the Most High. —Psalm 82.6

By your own right endeavors and God's grace, liberation of consciousness can be realized in your current incarnation. Your right endeavors allow rapid spiritual growth to naturally occur. Because of the inherent inclinations of Supreme Consciousness to express more freely as and through units of itself, the more receptive and responsive you are to its inclinations to be nurturing and transformative, the more evidence of grace you will have in your life. —Roy Eugene Davis

Reflect:

Can I accept the possibility of enlightenment in this lifetime? Can I welcome the responsibility enlightenment brings? Am I able to fully embrace it as my life purpose?

Christmas: Another Way

Being warned of God in a dream that they should not return to Herod,
they departed into their own country another way. —Matthew 2:12

Arriving on Christmas Day, let us reflect on the journey itself. The regal, wise ones come bearing their gifts of respect, insight, and devotion as they bow before Christ. This act signifies the illumined mind and transformed ego surrendering to the Christ Consciousness, the Higher Self. All components of the mind—thoughts, faculty of discernment, and ego-sense—have come into a harmonious, right relationship with the soul.

Viewed metaphysically, the journey of the wise men is an inner mystical journey through superconscious meditation to realize the Christ Consciousness within. They "follow the star in the east"—concentrate on the inner light perceived at the third eye—until awareness comes to rest in *Kutastha Chaitanya*, the unchanging, universal Christ, Krishna, or Buddha Consciousness. The wise men themselves represent our awakened faculty of discernment, the purified intellect in which the light of the true Self is revealed. In the yoga philosophy, we learn that once the *buddhi*, or faculty of discernment, is completely purified, the soul's radiant light fills it. No longer impeded by restlessness or false perception, the mental field is flooded with divine light, and realization dawns. This experience is called *dharma mega samadhi*—which translates as "the cloudburst of virtue."

Consciously abiding in our essential nature beyond thought or phenomena is the experience that is truly transforming. While inner perceptions of light, sound, or subtle energy may encourage our spiritual quest, only the direct experience of our essential nature transforms our knowing.

Once the wise men experience Christ, the story tells us they do not return to Herod. They do not return to the ego-based identity. The greatest gift of this holy day for every person is the gift of Self- and God-realization. This gift of grace, and this alone, brings new life. Those who discover it "return to their own country another way." A new life begins.

Practice:

Meditate more deeply today and intend to experience superconsciousness. Interiorize your attention by closing your eyes and focusing attention at the spiritual eye—slightly above and between the eyebrows. Imagine or feel as if you are breathing through this chakra center. With inhalation, inwardly listen to the word Om, and with exhalation, inwardly listen to the word God. Om, God.

When the mental field becomes quiet, let the mantra fall away but keep your inner gaze focused on the spiritual eye. Feel as if you are looking into the distance of internal space. If you perceive a field of blue light, a steady white, or gold light, gently focus your attention there. Remain inwardly attentive and relaxed. Be curious. Wait and watch in the silence, looking and listening within. Meditate for as long as you can stay alert.

Conclude this meditation by offering prayers for the entire world. Bless every person, everywhere on this holy day, with your wishes for their complete well-being and spiritual realization.

Contemplate:

The more conscious you are of the omnipresent Reality in which you abide, the easier it will be for you to know that all you need for your complete well-being is available to you. You will not have to ask for anything or use a lot of effort to accomplish your inspired purposes. You will live with graceful ease in harmonious accord with the rhythms of life. —Roy Eugene Davis

Breaking out is following your bliss pattern, quitting the old place, starting your hero journey, following your bliss. We must be willing to get rid of the life we've planned, so as to have the life that is waiting for us. —Joseph Campbell

Reflect:

Am I willing to go "another way" to embrace a new life?

Light on the Path

Lead us from the unreal to the Real,
Lead us from the darkness of ignorance to the light of truth,
Lead us from fear of death to awareness of immortality.
—Brihadaranyaka Upanishad

Our pilgrim's journey in the season of Advent reflects the universal soul passage from the confusion of ignorance to the light of truth. This awakening to our essential nature—Self- and God-realization—is the goal of Kriya Yoga. To know true freedom—liberation from the errors that bring suffering—and live skillfully in harmony with divine will are the natural expressions of a spiritually awakened life. This holy life is for everyone, and all are on their way to discover it. The mystical core of the world's religions, spiritual paths, and wisdom traditions are paths to this same goal: *Truth is One, the sages speak of it variously.*

When Paramahansa Yogananda brought the teachings of Kriya Yoga to the West, he carried an imperative from the yoga masters in the lineage who sent him—show the essential, spiritual harmony between the East and the West. To this end, he envisioned and established what he called churches of all religions—places of worship honoring all paths as various ways to the same goal of enlightenment.

Following the instructions given by my guru, Roy Eugene Davis, the first programs of our Center were Sunday worship services following the template and spirit established by his guru, Paramahansa Yogananda. That pattern has continued faithfully, since 1981, serving seekers of truth and lovers of God from many different religious backgrounds or none. Kriya Yoga is not a religion; it is a spiritual philosophy and practice for spiritually conscious living. It is a mystical path—a way of discovering the truth that is beyond words, thoughts, or beliefs. I have marveled to see the religiously diverse community gathered in our Temple of the Eternal Way to worship the One in silence.

Meditation is a portal to divine communion, and so is contemplation and ritual, the various ways we have to quiet the mind and open ourselves to realization. This *Meditator's Guide to Advent* is offered in that spirit. May your spiritual journey take you home, arriving joyfully to recognize and embrace your radiant Self.

About the Author

Yogacharya Ellen Grace O'Brian, M.A., is a Kriya Yoga teacher, writer, and spiritual director of the Center for Spiritual Enlightenment (CSE) with headquarters in San Jose, California, USA. CSE is a Kriya Yoga Meditation Center serving people from all faith backgrounds who are seeking Self- and God-realization. She was ordained to teach in 1982 by Roy Eugene Davis, a direct disciple of Paramahansa Yogananda who brought Kriya Yoga from India to the West. Yogacharya O'Brian has taught yoga philosophy and meditation practices for spiritually conscious living at retreats, spiritual centers, and conferences throughout the US and internationally for over four decades.

She is the author of several books on spiritual practice, including the award-winning book *the Jewel of Abundance: Finding Prosperity through the Ancient Wisdom of Yoga, Living the Eternal Way: Spiritual Meaning and Practice in Daily Life*, as well as three volumes of poetry including *The Moon Reminded Me*. She writes regularly for *Truth Journal* magazine, is the editor of *Enlightenment Journal*—a quarterly yoga magazine, hosts the *Kriya Yoga Today* podcast, and is the founder and frequent guest of *The Yoga Hour* podcast. Her teachings are available globally through several online courses, as well as freely accessible video and audio lessons.

Yogacharya O'Brian served as the Vice Chair of the Board of Trustees of the Parliament of the World's Religions and is a recipient of several community service awards, including the prestigious Mahatma Gandhi Award for the Advancement of Religious Pluralism by the Hindu American Foundation.

www.EllenGraceOBrian.com

About CSE

Center for Spiritual Enlightenment (CSE), founded in 1981, is a meditation center in the spiritual tradition of Kriya Yoga. The Center ministry welcomes people from all backgrounds who are seeking Self- and God-realization—a path to spiritually-conscious, fulfilled living in the world. The teachings offered at CSE have their origins in the ancient Vedas, which offer a universally applicable path for spiritual awakening relevant to our time. To realize the truth of our essential nature and live in the highest way is the goal of the path. Every day, both locally and globally, for over forty years, the CSE ministry has continued to offer spiritual teachings and practical support to all who are seeking a spiritually awakened life.

CSE World Headquarters is located in San Jose, California, where meditation instruction, Kriya Yoga teachings and initiation, worship services, hatha yoga classes, youth spiritual education, ministry services, and retreats are regularly offered. It is also the home of Meru Institute, founded in 1996 to train teachers and leaders in the Kriya Yoga tradition by offering educational programs in Yoga Studies, Ayurveda, and Community Ministry; a meditation garden that is open daily to the public; CSE Press; Lahiri House for private and small group meditation retreats; and Welcome Center and Bookshop.

CSE shares inspiration and teachings globally by offering daily and weekly programs, online classes, weekly podcast, daily email inspirations, publications, and outreach teachings. CSE affiliate centers and meditation groups are located in several US cities.

info@csecenter.org
CSEcenter.org

1146 University Avenue
San Jose, CA 95126
+1 408 283 0221

About CSE Press

Publications for Awakened Living

CSE Press was established in 1998 to provide an avenue for publication of the Kriya Yoga teachings offered by Yogacharya O'Brian. The first book published, *Living the Eternal Way: Spiritual Meaning and Practice for Daily Life* is still being offered two decades later. It remains the primary text for the *Live the Eternal Way* course, an introduction to the philosophy and practices of Kriya Yoga.

CSE Press has diversified over the years to include publication of an illustrated book for all ages titled *Once Before Time*, a creation story, three volumes of spiritual poetry, as well as several audio collections of inspirational messages on the spiritual classics such as the Bhagavad Gita, the Upanishads, Yoga Sutras of Patanjali, and the Gospel of Thomas.

CSE Press distributes books and other materials both nationally and internationally.

To subscribe to Daily Inspirations from Yogacharya O'Brian, via email:
visit: CSEcenter.org or
write to: info@csecenter.org